All my bones shall say...

AF624618

Charlotte Fletcher

BookLeaf Publishing

Presentation by *BookLeaf Publishing*

Web: www.bookleafpub.com

E-mail: info@bookleafpub.com

ISBN: 9789357443098

First edition 2023

ACKNOWLEDGEMENT

I want to thank my Mom and Dad for encouraging me with this writing, that it is a gift from God and to be used for His Glory, not my own. And of course, housing me, feeding me and watering me. For raising and training me in the ways I should go, even when I am old, I will not depart from it.

I thank my wonderful friends, Bryony R, Bethany S, Angela T, Zoe B and Mr and Mrs Turner for always encouraging me in the ways of the Lord and making me laugh along the way. I thank my Joshua. Who has always read my poetry, gave me the best encouragement, gave me confidence and been the optimist through all things. I know you love me as you love yourself, and I hope to encourage you as much as you have for me.

I thank Grace Community Church, Tipton. My family of eternity and I love you all so very much. You are my slice of heaven and I dont know how I would live without the encouragement, teaching and love of you all.

Finally, The Lord above. For He is the giver of all good things, and I will worship and praise Him all my days, young or old. For His blood rescued me, and my sins are white as snow.

PREFACE

Dear reader, I pray these poems bring you encouragement, joy and a new light to something on your mind. Whether you are new to Christ or a Christian for decades, I hope you enjoy these words.
These poems are greatly inspired by christian hymns, Psalms and my own journey of learning and realisation. It is easy to focus on one thing so much, everything else is known but forgotten. Some you may not be able to relate to you, but one may stay with you, and I implore you to pray and read the Bible for anything read which does so, or perhaps rip a page out and frame it for your bathroom wall.

I do hope the Lord speaks to you through these words. Know that everything you have suffered and faced has been faced by someone before, and the burden within has been carried and crossed out by our creator.

'So you must consider yourselves dead to sin and alive to God in Christ Jesus.' - Romans 6:11

When my King looks at me

When my king looks at me

He sees me in robes of white

Standing tall
Above it all

With light behind so bright

When my Lord looks at me

With Jesus tinted glasses

Crown my head
Sparkle red

With His blood that crowns the masses

When my God looks at me

Tears run down my face

Loved all along
Heard our song

With worship of His grace

When my Father looks at me

He sees His perfect work is done

Rose again
Descended then

Awaiting majesty shone

When our God, who looks at us

One day to call us high

His Glory shown
Each mind has known

Someday we all must die

When our King who calls to us

'Come now, for it is time'

He's sees my robes
Blind white He knows

'That's them, and they are mine'

Start and end

I was hoping to write a poem
That hit the perfect place
Like when the right chords are played
In the buildup of a songs pace

I was hoping for better
Obviously pathetic
I blamed others for what I lacked
But now see my expectations are unrealistic

Say I'm resting on God's Grace
But It's hardly resting really
That implies I'm calmly sleeping
But in reality I landed face first looking silly

Hitting my shin of the table
I squeeled and did it again
To make sure it hurt
As much as I thought it did back then

I broke a toe, cut my lip
Showed a smile in the street
Attempted prayer with the same feeling
I did three years ago when it was fresh and
sweet

Gods' grace, His Mercy
His kindness, my hope
Hitting the speed gravity lets
And I land, in grace. No longer can cope

Tell myself 'I'm done!'
That's it's no more na, yav 'ad enough
My pride climbs my ladder
And poof I'm off again feeling rough

It's repetitive this poem
Like sin, there's a theme

I can't stop myself but
In repentance and prayer know I'm redeemed

Christ is my happiness
I fear cause sometimes I have none
These habits, speech, actions vary
But again I get up and again I pray through the
Son

So Lord, if you hear me
Oh how can I say that
Of course you do
I know, I honestly do

That you can forgive me for being me
Help me to love you
Your my hope, friend, judge, and saviour
I will worship you from then until forever

Yesterday, today, tomorrow, I will change

Your Spirit is working to improve me in my
failed days

So here I stand
Constantly repenting, struggling, recovering
Christ Jesus, my Lord and my God
He has done it. Forgiven us, through his life and
suffering

I encourage, if you face plant too
To pray and recover Like we all do

Through the one way to grace that we can get
Christ Jesus our hope, my hope and rest

Scripture Part 1

It's a walk

The Bible and stories

Where we can wonder

Get lost in journeys

Start at the start

The earth and heavens are dawned

Your footprint in the sand

No man before ever formed

Carry on through

From the beautiful to the new old

Where man disobeys

And they become wild

Careful there!

Many plagues to suffer

Watch your step of locusts

But the frogs are tougher

See the people

The kings they form

The prophets fortold

And the empires that are torn

Watch the Red Sea split

The wars that lost and prevailed

See the Moabite woman

Working hard in a field

Look there's an axe in the water

See how it floats

Amazing things happen here

But no one good ever gloats

The wars continue here

You can see the sin taking hold

It's dark and dangerous

But we don't need to be told

The history continues

We're glad to have you here

There vital these beginnings

They wait for the saviour to appear

Take a rest now

Take a sleep, think it through

It points to one man

And Isaiah knows it too

Join me in the morning

Awake and ready to see

More blessings and mercy

And all true. I guarantee!

Scripture Part 2

Welcome to the new path!

Let us take a dive right in

But maybe you should step in faith

Walk on water like Christ did

Whoops. Spoilers.

We haven't quite got there yet

But you know in the beginning was the Word

Who's already paid our debt

Four men here

They write their account of what they saw

But they're account could not contain

The wonders of God and more

God was born of a virgin, Mary

Sin was not inherited to Him

In such a low, poor place

To show wealth means nothing

Swven miracles were performed

He fullfilled every prophecy wrote in old

Baptised in His spirit

It must have been such a sight to behold!

Peter, Pilot, and Paul

All vital of our Messiahs' travel

His life, teaching, death, life again

The stories now to unravel

Now Peter let us down

Cmon, lets be honest

We all say 'Why Peter Why!'

But we do this too! We break every promise!

None are good

We've all fallen short

The only good is Christ in us

Now dead to sin, our transgressions naught

The New Testament is split

Past, present, and future

Paul's letters to churches

Are our present lecture

Revelation comes

The end of the end!

Where Christs feet walk the Earth

So follow His lead we recommend!

The Earth will disintegrate

Dark nights and dark days

Devil's reign of terror

Where evil always pays

But those in Christ

Gods Love and Spirit

We will rise again in the new new

For who were committed

The future praises the God of Israel

The dead rise like a shining silver birch

We are clothed in blinding white

We are His bride, we are the church!

Wrote for Ann

Our Lord our saviour
The God who created
Made us in His image and behaviour
To become hated

The poor people of the world
So absorbed and distant
I live my life to spread His word
But they never listen

The graciousness he provides
The daily miracle that is He
For us to breathe and once alive
To find Him and in paradise be

I will live and learn and sanctify
Though hard as it may seem
I will tell my friends and testify
In my church we are a team

Scripture can provide for us

Can cut deep like a shard
Though study and listening seems effortless
It's hearing which is hard

Our Lord our saviour
The God and King who died
His love and grace will never waver
My soul is forever satisfied

O, what to write when there is He

Oh what to write of when there is He
Son of Mary
In all His glory
He somehow chose me
With my faults and insecurity
He willingly defends me
Though I fail daily
I am reliant on his mercy
Oh what to write of when there is He
The creator, physician, holy
who can heal thee
or let my body be
though sin is a trap of heresy
forever we will wholehearted
Lean on His grace and be free
The future He can foresee
Eventually
He will be calmed of his jealousy
For we will be heavenly
Will definitely
Happily
Worship thee
In perfect company
The great Lord of you and me

Say now life's a tragedy
Understanding sin faintly
For unbelievers a catastrophe
They look not to the story
Wrote by the Spirit Holy
Of His decency
They ignore it dangerously
I implore thee
Do not dismiss me
It's not just empathy
It is a righteous courtesy
To share the love of He
Who died for you and me
Who walked across the sea
Who suffered severely
I praise He
King of my King I Worship thee
And with thine eyes I'll see
Heavens golden walk way beside He
Eventually
I'll wait unnervingly
Check my watch religiously
But now, I unintentionally
Displease God and me
Forgive thee
I fail daily
I'll lean on your mercy
Oh, what to write when there is He

Proud

Dare we stand proud to say we did it right
All my kind words, gentle care or mercy
Could I, shoulders back, claim decieved height
To walk into paradise, heart worthy

Dare we tower over God himself
Exclaiming majesty, works or glory
Given money, smiles or flowers on a shelf
'I did it alone' they say. 'None were before me'

Proud one, do know, the peacock also dies
It's feathers do not stop time passing fast
You will stand before the throne of justice
There, naked, no claim under just wrath

Please hear the plea of Christianity
The church calls to lead you right
Humble yourself as a sinner with vanity
And you will, as the rest of us, be seen
Holy in His sight

Test of faith

How old were you when you were saved?
Did it make a difference in your life?
Have you been sanctified and changed?
Do you look differently on strife?
These trials are made to test you
In that there is no doubt
You grow spiritually and emotionally
From the world you will stand out
We know that Job was righteous
Yet he had the worst of all
His family were living in paradise
While he was begging for the Lord's Call
Riches you need not but
God Gives this to some
Remember your creator in the days of your
youth before the days of trouble come
A poor man can be saved by grace
A rich man can be lost
Though remember we're all rich and all poor at
some cost
So pray! I beg you!
Pray because you can
You have the joy of calling Him Father
And see where you land
Rest your worry on Him

He will deliver us from evil and then
Always in His kingdom
His power and His glory
For ever and ever
Amen

Learning more and more about myself each day

My Lord, my God
I come before you a sinner
Unstable in my ways
Just lately I find myself doubting these days
Though I don't doubt your love or mercy
I just expect the day to come
Where at your gates its disappointment I see
I cannot expect hugs and trumpets
Joy songs of angels harps
I picture a side hug, half smile
Not angry, but upset and sharp
I wait days to pray when I shouldn't
To give Him time to cool off
I must learn of your instant grace
For it is finished with Christ on the cross
Forgive me, please
Love me like I'm new
I'll continue
In Spirit, in love, in mercy
This I will do

Trumpet when I died

I heard the trumpet music when I died
Beats on beat was like-
A thunder clap within a hurricane peak

The body felt no pain
As my mind gave way
Floating steadily
As the Son of Man guided me

The dead buried the dead that day-
That my shell would stay in Earth
I continued in my journey
Where my steps did not sink in turf

With the blinding glory
Of heavens palace holy
I walked in the fields of light
Out of the shadows of the valley

To the tune of 'be thou my vision'

Family or friends they
Speak of thy past old
Knowing you're here with thee
Your word foretold
Here my heart sits kind
In peace or despair
Knowing your promise
I'll meet with thee there

Father forgive me
For past, future, now
Drowning with tears I
Call for mercy new
Jesus my heart be
Yours forevermore
Save me life steady
Eternity sure

Stepping though day time
Night sleep and again

Guiding through Spirit
Our eyes see clear then
We are but travellers
No world which to stay
Home made in heaven
As Earth pass away

Lord give me wisdom
To sing as your will
Worship, praise, worthy
Your holiness still
Time after all time
You're always the same
Forgiveness is given
Bestowed once again

Resting on your hope
Christ always remains
No work b'fore your throne
Which I can forclaim
Falling and sleeping
Your word keeps me sure
Your Spirit is living
Our ruler of all

It was all for us

On that day

The dreaded day

Something awful was to happen

Though with His death

The humiliation they saw

And a pain they could not fathom

The sun did not shine

Pitch black dawn

Earth wore funeral attire

She mourned the death of her creator

The sun watched the Son become higher

For three hours darkness reigned

While the Light was being dimm'd

The sun rose again

As did the Son

But with the world's desires untrimm'd

To sit to the right

Of The Father Himself

Waiting to one day soon return

I pray you listen

I pray you hear

But importantly I pray you learn

There's one

There's one to forgive

There's one to forget

Perhaps I'm not both

But I will try my best

There is one who is correct

There is one who is sound

I want to be that

But I am too proud

There is one who is true

There is one who can preach

I can talk to you and tell

Of all the good things

There is one who can change me

There is one who can edit

So I try to notice when

The sin takes over and I let it

There is someone who is good

Someone like the sun

God they call him

Jesus,

Yeah, he's the one

He's the giver

Of all good things

Unfortunately I'm the not one

That this poem sings

Though I can try, I can change

I can forgive and forget

With The Holy Spirits work

I can be my best yet

With tomorrow and tomorrow

I wake and awake

To pray and praise

the rest of my life is at stake

For now I forgive

One day I'll forget

And in His name

I will be my best

For your bathroom wall

My friend, my friend
Hear my plea when I say
The sky is falling
A decision needs to be made today

They say tomorrow never comes
But your living in it right now!
You may not wake in the morning
You may pass away somehow

I encourage you to speak to us
You know the Lord is there
He's ready to forgive
Just believe in Christ, repent in prayer

I know it sounds scary
It may even wound your pride
But humility is humanity
With God there's no need to hide

He made us in His form
There is nothing he has not seen or known
If your heart receives the truth
It's because you have been shown

So sit down with us
We will make you a cuppa tea or two
We can tell you all about the word
Which made us Christians new

Now don't get confused
We still fail sometimes too
No one here is perfect
But we have learnt what is true

One day in the future
We want you at our feast
All kinds will be there
From the richest to the least

So look to the cross
Understand your past fall
For now we have the Father, Son and Spirit
Who is ready to forgive all.

The Sand

Standing in the sand
The snake bites my foot
Weaknesses, shaking
I'm not the only one
I couldn't crush it
The heel infected
I stand to this day
Robes on me dirty
To look up and see
A cross held up distantly
His blood
A puddle
It cured thee
The venom drew out
I'm free
Standing in the sand
The snake bites my foot
Checks it's watch and waits
For us to bleed, fall, cut
He's waiting his turn
The creature on its belly
But the golden shining white of Jesus
Has cured us all
All with faith to see

Your praise matters

When singing we lift our voices to Him
Our natural instrument given kindly
Whether in tune or forced, our heart within
He knows, He hears, praising He will find me

When praying we may close our hands tightly
Perhaps you kneel or bow beside your bed
Gathered in His name in spirit rightly
The Lord kind hears and provides all you said

What or who we all worship is vital
A golden calf will not amend our days
Sing and pray to the God of the Bible
Our King, our creator in all good ways.

Sonnet

Sometimes we're looked at funny as if old
As if our thoughts and truth are out of date
We may receive a comment, we may get told
There is no God for science evident

Looking down on you, no drink, no gossip
Dress modest, don't swear, abide by old law
They judge for judging, care only of profit
They know the way they say, deceived for sure

And yet, our hearts know the way right and true
To love the Lord, my God I will continue

Look at this!

Look at this! Look at this! All blessings given
Things considered basic or essential
Wanting more we thrive our ambition
Many hidden somewhat confidential

Living in breathing state I walk my day
Breathe taken and exhaled without thought
Some negatives I foolish believe outweigh
Cannot outshine the joy of future He bought

Difficulty seeing at time in pain
This roof over my head with hot water bath
Upon resting allow me to count in rain
The kindly given love, no sign of wrath

My heart be thankful, understanding, grateful
For your family loves you and gain them daily
In prayer stay continually faithful
Until that day in glory I will be

Oh rest still my heart

Oh rest still my heart
You are troubled to no end
You have prayed to rest
And rest you will spend
Remember you're dead to sin
In Christs righteousness your loved
You cannot out sin grace
No matter how deep the mud
Romans 6:11
Read this and week with joy
Lose the anxiety and fear
The evil one likes to destroy
Be encouraged now, sinless sinner
Your white coat smile makes you shimmer.

The plan

Was this all planned?
My birth, breath, baptism
The plan from the start
Your creation created in your wisdom

You're the masterpiece artist
The first painter of The Last Supper
From the dawn of existence
To all that Christ has to suffer

Planned beautifully
Executed perfectly
There's nothing man can do
To fix our relationship personally

We cannot rely on works
They cannot make us merry
But your only role in salvation
Is the sin that made it necessary

Paradise: a worded painting

In Paradise
In Heaven
He resides in a palace
The flowers
The sunshine
He drinks from golden chalice

The waters
Living waters
It's clear no reflections
Cool and fresh
No memory of afflictions

Blue skies
Clouds white
Each one has bright shine lining
No storm
No sea
We're not separated by timing

His kingdom
Our heaven
Earth without the fall
We imagine
Future there

Our expectations He exceeds them all

A chandelier
Without celing
Stars he counted now looking at us
His intention
His will
He said He loved us, and He does.

It all came
Together in death
Here there's no need to rebuild
Trees in bloom
Eden eternal summer
The past has finally been fulfilled

www.ingramcontent.com/pod-product-compliance
Lightning Source LLC
Chambersburg PA
CBHW051740130826
49812CB00033B/936
* 9 7 8 9 3 5 7 4 4 3 0 9 8 *